Road Signs, Airlines, And Stars

A Journey From Advent To Christmas

Cynthia E. Cowen

CSS Publishing Company, Inc., Lima, Ohio

ROAD SIGNS, AIRLINES, AND STARS

For more information about CSS Publishing Company resources, visit our website at www.csspub.com or e-mail us at custserv@csspub.com or call (800) 241-4056.

ISBN 0-7880-1910-4
PRINTED IN U.S.A.

I wish to dedicate this resource to my son, Justin Edwin Paul Cowen, who is a trooper at bringing to life the many characters I have created for my youth programs over the years. What a gift he was in making this resource turn out so well! Be it driving youth to a Christmas party and watching all the road signs, or playing Joseph caring for his precious cargo on the way to Bethlehem, or running the camcorder to record my college youth, Maria Gibson, Erin Donovan, Angela Freeman, and Stephanie Pitts, my All Star cast for Christmas Eve worship, he has always been there for me. How blessed I have been to have youth who love Jesus and are open to sharing their enthusiasm with others. And I am especially blessed to have a caring and outgoing son like Justin who lights up my heart with his joy for life and the Lord.

Table Of Contents

Our Advent Journey

Foreword

Use this creative resource as a mid-week Advent service put on by youth, an intergenerational Advent program, a Sunday school program, or a weekend worship service. Journey with youth as they pick up friends and road signs along the way to their Christmas party at church. Substitute the names of your youth for those in the script.

Prayers, lessons, bulletin, and skit make this a resource that youth can easily lead. Program coordinator can contact the local highway department for road signs or make individual signs for the skit. This is an exciting program with a salvation message that is revealed as youth take an Advent journey and are confronted along the way with the real meaning of Advent.

Bulletin

Our Advent Journey
Mid-week Advent Service

Prelude

Welcome And Announcements

Call To Worship Youth
Leader: Let us rise. We come this night preparing our hearts to receive Jesus the Christ once again. The Light of Christ is shining from this place. May our lives reflect God's love to a world in darkness. Come, let us rejoice in Jesus who sets us free to be beacons of hope to others.
Congregation: Appear in our midst, Lord Jesus. Amen.

Opening Hymn: "Rejoice, Rejoice, Believers"
  Rejoice, rejoice, believers,
  And let your lights appear;
  The evening is advancing,
  And darker night is near.
  The bridegroom is arising
  And soon is drawing nigh.
  Up, pray and watch and wrestle;
  At midnight comes the cry.

  Our hope and expectation,
  O Jesus, now appear;
  Arise, O Sun so longed for,
  O'er this benighted sphere.
  With hearts and hands uplifted,
  We plead, O Lord, to see
  The day of earth's redemption
  That sets your people free!

Litany Of Preparation

Leader: Lord God, you looked down upon your earth and your heart was grieved.

Congregation: We need your love in our world, O Lord.

Leader: It was your plan to save us from our sins, Lord God.

Congregation: Forgive us our sins, O Lord.

Leader: Jesus is your plan to reveal your love that will save us.

Congregation: God's great love became flesh in a child called Immanuel, God with us.

Leader: Child of Bethlehem, your journey through life was to demonstrate God's love for all people.

Congregation: Immanuel is with us on our journey.

Leader: Jesus, your journey from the manger to the cross set us free.

Congregation: Prince of Peace, you reconciled us to the Father by your birth and death.

Leader: Wonderful Counselor, Almighty God, Everlasting Father, you call us this Advent season to prepare our hearts to house the Savior of the world.

Congregation: Holy Spirit, birth Jesus anew in our lives. Amen.

Prayer Of The Day   Youth

Leader: Dear God, please help us to prepare our hearts to welcome your one and only Son, Jesus, into our lives this Advent season. Forgive us our sins and help us to remember you every day of our lives. In Jesus' name,

Congregation: Amen.

Return To The Lord, Your God

First Reading: Isaiah 40:3-5 (CEV)   Youth

Someone is shouting: "Clear a path in the desert! Make a straight road for the Lord our God. Fill in the valleys; flatten every hill and mountain. Level the rough and rugged ground. Then the glory of the Lord will appear for all to see. The Lord has promised this!"

Second Reading: Colossians 1:15-18 (CEV)   Youth

Christ is exactly like God, who cannot be seen. He is the first-born Son, superior to all creation. Everything was created by him, everything in heaven and on earth, everything seen and unseen, including all forces and powers, and all rulers and authorities. All things were created by God's Son, and everything was made for him. God's Son was before all else, and by him everything is held together. He is the head of his body, which is the church. He is the very beginning, the first to be raised from death, so that he would be above all others.

Special Music: "Come, Thou Long-Expected Jesus" or other selection

Gospel Reading: Luke 1:5-17 (CEV)   Youth

When Herod was king of Judea, there was a priest by the name of Zechariah from the priestly group of Abijah. His wife Elizabeth was from the family of Aaron. Both of them were good people and pleased the Lord God by obeying all that he had commanded. But they did not have children. Elizabeth could not have any, and both Zechariah and Elizabeth were already old. One day Zechariah's group of priests were on duty, and he was serving God as a priest. According to the custom of the priests, he had been chosen to go into the Lord's temple that day and to burn incense, while the people stood outside praying.

All at once an angel from the Lord appeared to Zechariah at the right side of the altar. Zechariah was confused and afraid when he saw the angel. But the angel told him:

"Don't be afraid, Zechariah! God has heard your prayers. Your wife Elizabeth will have a son, and you must name him John. His birth will make you very happy, and many people will be glad. Your son will be a great servant of the Lord. He must never drink wine or beer, and the power of the Holy Spirit will be with him from the time he is born. John will lead many people in Israel to turn back to the Lord their God. He will go ahead of the Lord with the same power and spirit that Elijah had. And because of John, parents will be more thoughtful of their children. And people who now disobey God will begin to think as they ought to. That is how John will get people ready for the Lord."

Zechariah said to the angel, "How will I know this is going to happen? My wife and I are both very old."

The angel answered: "I am Gabriel, God's servant, and I was sent to you to tell you this good news. You have not believed what I have said. So you will not be able to say a thing until all this happens. But everything will take place when it is supposed to."

Congregational Hymn: "Prepare The Royal Highway"
Prepare the royal highway;
The King of kings is near!
Let ev'ry hill and valley
A level road appear!
Then greet the King of glory,
Foretold in sacred story:
Refrain: Hosanna to the Lord,
For he fulfills God's Word!

His is no earthly kingdom;
It comes from heav'n above.
His rule is peace and freedom
And justice, truth, and love.
So let your praise be sounding
For kindness so abounding:
Refrain

Skit: A Night Time Journey

Special Music

Reflection   Pastor

Offering

11

Prayers of the Church
Leader: Lord in your mercy,
Congregation: Hear our prayer.

The Lord's Prayer

Our Father, who art in heaven,
   hallowed be thy name.
Thy kingdom come,
   thy will be done,
   on earth as it is in heaven.
Give us this day our daily bread;
   and forgive us our trespasses,
   as we forgive those who trespass against us;
   and lead us not into temptation,
   but deliver us from evil.
For thine is the kingdom, and the power, and the glory, forever and ever. Amen.

Benediction

Leader: Go in the name of the Father whose love birthed the Son and through the Holy Spirit the Word became flesh and came to live among us. Be filled with God's mercy, Christ's love, and the Holy Spirit's anointing.
Congregation: We open our hearts to your love, King of glory. Amen.

Closing Hymn: "Good Christian Friends, Rejoice"
   Good Christian friends, rejoice,
   With heart and soul and voice;
   Give ye heed to what we say:
   Jesus Christ is born today;
   Ox and ass before him bow,
   And he is in the manger now.
   Christ is born today!
   Christ is born today!

Good Christian friends, rejoice
With heart, and soul, and voice;
Now ye hear of endless bliss:
Jesus Christ was born for this!
He has ope'd the heavenly door,
And we are blessed for evermore.
Christ was born for this!
Christ was born for this!

Good Christian friends, rejoice
With heart and soul and voice;
Now ye need not fear the grave;
Jesus Christ was born to save!
Calls you one and calls you all
To gain his everlasting hall.
Christ was born to save!
Christ was born to save!

Dismissal
Leader: Go in peace to worship the Savior of the world.
Congregation: We go to celebrate our Lord Jesus Christ.

Skit

A Night Time Journey

Skit Helps

Stage setting:

Chairs set up behind railing or a constructed cardboard car.

Left Side: Table with telephone.

Right Side: Table with telephone and clock.

Props:

Car made from cardboard box around twelve chairs.

Signs for each of the carriers — Contact your local county road commission and they may make them up for you or have extras.

Table with steering wheel set up (Fisher Price toy).

Skit Participants/Props: 16 youth

John: Wears Santa hat, cordless telephone, clock. May change all other names of participants to fit your youth group, but keep this one "John."

Justin: Wears Santa hat, uses steering wheel set up, money for gas.

Ernie: Wears Santa hat, pretends to use gas hose.

Kayla: Wears hat and scarf. Pulls water bottle out later for deer. Sits next to Justin.

Deer: Prop sign — Deer Crossing. Wears antlers and a beeping red nose. Carries a long list which she hands to Justin.

Rough Road Ahead Sign: Carries Rough Road sign. (All youth may put their scripts on back of signs.)

Stop Sign: Carries Stop sign. Jamie

Right Turn Sign: Carries Right Turn sign. — Danielle

Yield Sign: Carries Yield sign. Allison

Jimmy: Wears hat and carries bucket of water.

Child #1 and Child #2: Carry Children at Play sign.

14

School Zone: Carries School Zone sign.
No Passing: Carries No Passing sign.
Reserved Parking Sign: Carries Reserved Parking sign.
Music Person(s): Wears a Christmas hat and/or sign around neck: "God Rocks!"
Sings: "On Jordan's Banks The Baptist's Cry" (v. 1); "On Jordan's Banks The Baptist's Cry" (v. 2); "Joy To The World" (v. 1); "Oh, Come, Little Children" (v. 1).
Produces a sign during the Time Of Silence: "Advent — take time to think!"

Presentation

The parts in the skit do not need to be memorized. Youth who have road signs can tape their parts to the back of the sign and read them. Others can have their scripts in folders or just hold them. Youth today are not keen on memorization. But if your youth can do it, great! Make this a fun journey for them, not a trial.

Speakers may use the lectern microphone system.

————————

(John is seated stage right; Justin is seated stage left)

John: "Oh, come, all ye faithful, joyful and triumphant. Oh, come ye, oh come ye to Bethlehem ..." I love this time of the year. Advent: a time to prepare for Jesus' birth once more. And speaking of that preparation ... *(Looks at clock and picks up portable telephone)* I'd better call Justin and make sure he hits the highway to pick up the kids for our Christmas party tonight. I'd hate to go through all this preparation and have nobody come. *(Makes ringing sounds)* Ring, ring. Ring, ring.

Justin: *(Answers telephone)* Hello! Who's calling on this calm and wintry night?

John: Merry Christmas, Justin! It's John here. Are you ready? Are you prepared for your Advent journey?

Justin: I'm going on a journey? Is this good news?

John: Of course it is. Remember I talked to you the other night at youth group about picking up kids for our Christmas party?

Justin: Yeah, it seems to me you mentioned it.

John: Well?

Justin: Yeah? What?

John: Well, are you going to do it?

Justin: Do what?

John: Pick up the kids! I've done a lot of preparation to get set for this night. The food's ordered, the soda's in the refrig, postcards went out, and I've even called everyone to remind them. But I need you to start dashing through the town to pick up those who can't get here by themselves. Okay?

Justin: Okay, since you have done a lot of the advance work, I guess I can do my part. Who do you want me to zero in on?

John: Well, I need you to pick up Kayla, then Jimmy. If you find any extras along the way, invite them to come along.

Justin: Gottcha! Just have to put some gas in the car, and I'll be set. See you in about an hour.

(John leaves. Justin enters in his pretend car)

Justin: And away we go!

Ernie: *(Enters to fill up tank)* Hi, Justin! Can I help you?

Justin: Fill it up, Ernie. I'm about to begin a journey into the night. Hey, you coming to youth group tonight?

Ernie: Wouldn't miss it, Justin! There's more to life than filling gas tanks. I really enjoy being with Christian friends. I need to tell all of you what Jesus has done in my life lately. In fact, I'm so *pumped* I'd love to tell you right now. Got a minute?

Justin: Not right now, Ernie. Let's save it 'til later. Okay? Here's the money I owe you. *(Hands Ernie money)* I'm off to pick up Kayla and Jim. See you at church.

Ernie: Have a safe journey, Justin. See you later. May the Lord be with you. *(Leaves stage)*

Justin: I'm out of here. What's with everyone lately? This season sure seems to affect people in a strange way. My mom's one of them. I need some music to accompany me on this trip. *(Pretends to fuss with radio)*

Music Person: *(Sings)* "On Jordan's Banks the Baptist's Cry" (v. 1)

Justin: Oh, great! Who messed with my dial? Must have been my mom again. She's really gotten "churchy" on me lately. All that "God loves you." "Jesus is Lord!" "Open your heart, Justin. Let the Spirit come in." Maybe she's going through the change of life. Anyway, here I am at Kayla's. *(Pretends to honk horn)* Honk, honk. Hey, Kayla, come on, let's get on with our Advent journey.

Kayla: *(Runs out and gets into car)* Our what?

Justin: Our Advent journey. John's got all the preparations ready. He's at church waiting for us. It's our mission to collect the souls we find this night.

Kayla: Aren't we sounding "churchy"! Let me tune some music in for our journey. *(Pretends to fuss with radio)*

Music Person: *(Sings)* "On Jordan's Banks The Baptist's Cry" (v. 2)

Kayla: Hey? What's that station? K-Rock it ain't. Isn't that your favorite?

Justin: I know, I know. My mom must have fussed with the dial. You know I don't get into that Christian stuff that deep. Youth group, going to church, and saying a prayer for a test. We don't need to become *radical* about our faith.

Kayla: Well, what if I told you I've gotten *radical*. I'd like to share my experience with you. *(Holds up hand and shouts)* Hey! Watch out! There's a deer.

Deer: *(Bounds out)* Halt!

Justin: A talking deer! And look at that nose! It's blinking! You aren't Rudolph, are you?

Deer: You mean that red-nosed, story book reindeer that saved Santa's Christmas ride?

Justin: Yeah, that's the one. Are you the savior of Christmas Eve?

Deer: You've got to be kidding. I thought you were a Christian. It says so here on my list. *(Pulls out list and gives to Justin)*

Justin: *(Takes the list)* What's this? Category — Lukewarm Christians: Justin Smith. Me? Lukewarm?

Kayla: *(Takes list from Justin)* Look! Here I am! On the first page — Radical for Jesus! Kayla Jones.

Deer: Yep! You moved from lukewarm to radical when you went to that last retreat. Remember? You said a prayer and asked the Holy Spirit to increase your love for Jesus.

Kayla: It was such a moving night. I felt such peace, such joy!

Justin: Don't get "churchy" on me now, Kayla. You're beginning to sound more and more like my mom. Let's get going or we'll be late for the youth group Christmas party.

Deer: Party! Can I come? I haven't been to a real good Christian Christmas party in a long time. Do you sing songs? Play games? Have pizza?

Justin: Deer don't eat pizza. And I don't know what John has prepared. But if you'd like to come, hop in the back. We're on our way to pick up another lost soul.

Deer: *(Gets in behind Justin)* Oh, I know all about lost souls. Haven't you ever heard about me in the Bible?

Kayla: You're mentioned in the Bible?

Deer: Why, yes! In the Old Testament — Psalm 42. How about a long drink of spring water? I sure am thirsty.

Kayla: Here, have a swig from my water bottle. *(Passes water bottle to deer who drinks)* What's that passage say, dear deer?

Deer: *(Passes bottle back)* Thanks for the drink. Why that passage talks about our longing for God. The psalmist says: "As a deer gets thirsty for streams of water, I truly am thirsty for you, my God. In my heart, I am thirsty for you, the living God. When will I see your face?" (Psalm 42:1-2 CEV). Hey, Justin! *(Justin, Kayla, and Deer jump as if hitting a bump)* Watch out! Don't you see that sign?

Rough Road Ahead Sign: *(Hops in front of car and points at Justin)* Halt! Meet God face-to-face. You're in for some rough rounds, young man, unless you stop being lukewarm and become radical for Jesus.

Justin: This journey is getting a little confronting. Let me see your credentials.

Rough Road: Well, I come straight from our first lesson tonight. Isaiah said, "Get the road ready for the Lord! Make a straight path for him." You see, God sent me to you tonight to straighten out your crooked paths and smooth out the rough roads. Then you will see the saving power of God.

Justin: So, I suppose you want to hop on board this vehicle like our deer friend, too?

Rough Road: Well, with me on board, your road will be much easier to travel.

Kayla: Come on, Justin. Let God take control of the wheel of your life.

Justin: Hey! I'm doing just fine being in control of my life. But I suppose having God on your side, the journey might be a little smoother. Hop in, RR. Take a seat next to the thirsty deer. We've got to get moving here. Let's put the pedal to the metal and go! *(All say, "Varooom!")* See if you can get some music to set our feet a dancing, Kayla!

Kayla: I'll see what I can do. *(Fusses with pretend radio)*

Music Person: *(Sings)* "Joy To The World" (v. 1)

Justin: Now I can relate to that — *joy!* Isn't that what everyone is after?

Kayla: But it's joy down deep in your heart, Justin. Only the joy that Jesus can give.

Deer and Rough Road: *(Sing)* "I've got that joy, joy, joy, joy, down in my heart. Down in my heart, down in my heart. I've got that joy, joy, joy, joy, down in my heart. Down in my heart today."

(Optional: Music Person can help sing song also)

Justin: *(Turns around to back seat singers)* Quiet down! I hear you! I hear you!

Stop Sign: *(Jumps out)* But have you really heard the Spirit's voice, Justin?

Justin: Whoa! And what Advent character might you be? I recognize the Stop Sign, but what's your relationship to this night?

Stop Sign: Well, you know your friend, John?

Justin: Yeah! He's out there making all our preparations.

Stop Sign: Well, John the Baptist, the one your Gospel talked about, was like your John of today. Just as your friend John has made a lot of preparations because he loves you, that John of the Bible went about the kingdom with God's love preparing the people for Jesus' advent into their lives. But his message was a little hard for a lot of souls to receive.

Kayla: Why was that?

Stop Sign: Because he said, "Repent! Turn back to God, and your sins will be forgiven." In other words, stop doing what you know is wrong. Tell God you want to stop sinning. Only Jesus can forgive the past, help you journey through the rough roads of life in the present, and ...

Rough Road: Hey! You got that! With God in control, the crooked paths will be made smooth and those who turn from sin will be forgiven by the grace of God.

Deer: And ... God will give you eternal life as you believe in his Son.

Justin: Okay, I hear you back seat drivers. Let me think about it. Hop in, Stop Sign. *(Stop Sign takes place behind Deer and Rough Road)* We're on our way again. But don't turn that music on. I need time to think.

(Music Person produces sign: "Advent — take time to think!" Observe a few moments of silence)

Kayla: Watch out! There's another sign from God right on the road to Jimmy's.

Right Turn Sign: *(Jumps in front of the car. Youth with Yield sign stands next to her) Right!* Not *left*, but *right*, and God's call to you this Advent season is: "Turn *right!*"

Rough Road Sign: Hit the brakes, Justin. Let's get it *right* with God.

Right Turn Sign: *Right!* Isaiah says, "Whether you turn to the right or to the left, you will hear a voice saying, 'This is the road! Now follow it' " (Isaiah 30:21 CEV).

Justin: You say, "Right Turn," but this other sign says, "Yield."

Yield Sign: *Right!* God's offering you an invitation this Advent season to return to him. So, don't be *left* out! Hear Isaiah's words: "I, the Lord, invite you to come and talk it over. Your sins are scarlet red, but they will be whiter than snow or wool" (Isaiah 1:18 CEV).

Deer: Justin, God is calling, and he wants *ewe*. Baah!

Justin: Cute, Deer. Keep that sheep stuff in the barn though.

Kayla: But she's right, Justin.

Right Turn Sign: *Right*! Let's go right, Justin. *(Points the sign to the right)*

Justin: I hear you! Sheep follow their shepherd. People stop their sinning and yield their wills to God's.

Yield Sign: Hey, I think he's got it! Remember Joseph when he found out Mary was pregnant, and she told him it was by the Holy Spirit?

Justin: Yes, that was a big story to believe.

Yield Sign: But Mary yielded her will to God's when the angel Gabriel appeared. She said, "I am the Lord's servant! Let it happen as you have said" (Luke 1:38 CEV).

Stop Sign: And when an angel appeared to Joseph in a dream, he stopped doubting and believed, yielding his will to God's taking Mary as his wife. Today God calls each of us to stop and turn to him.

Yield Sign: And to yield control of our lives to the Holy Spirit so we will be blessed.

Justin: Okay! Hop in the back. It's a good thing I took my dad's van instead of my car. We are getting mighty crowded on this journey into the night. *(Right Turn and Yield enter car)*

Kayla: Hey, there's Jimmy, and he's looking for us!

(Jimmy appears before the group carrying a bucket of water)

Justin: Hi, guy! What's up?

Jimmy: I might ask you the same thing. Who are all these extras you've picked up in this night adventure?

Justin: It'd take a long time to explain, but John's waiting for us at church. He's done a lot of preparation and is expecting us to show up.

Jimmy: Well, I'm set. He just called and told me to bring this bucket of water. Said we had a very thirsty crew coming, and he wanted me to be ready.

Deer: I can understand that. So, what's keeping us here?

Justin: Nothing! Let's hit the road. *(Jimmy jumps into the car)* How about some traveling music?

Kayla: If you're ready. We've only been able to get one signal, and it's been heavenly music. Are you ready for the signal that God's sending to us this night?

Jimmy: I guess so. Let's hear it.

Music Person: *(Sings)* "Oh, Come, Little Children" (v. 1)

Jimmy: Hey, I'm not a little child. I'm turning sixteen this month. In fact, the day after Christmas.

Children at Play Sign: *(Child #1 and Child #2 jump in front of car and together sing)* Happy birthday to you! Happy birthday to you! Happy birthday, dear child of God, happy birthday to you!

Child #1: Jesus tells us to come as little children to him ... and that means to have the faith of a child no matter how old you are.

Child #2: Can we come on board? I think you all need to have more fun in life. Christmas is a time for love and peace and laughter. What a joy we have in Jesus! *(Enters car along with Child #1)*

Jimmy: Have we entered the Twilight Zone?

Justin: You might say that. This Advent journey into the night has really been strange. But you know, since we've started off, I feel a softening in my heart.

Jimmy: Watch out! There's another sign, and it's headed our way!

School Zone: *(Stops the car)* Hey, guys! You're almost there! Remember me? I'm all those things you've already been exposed to as you've traveled this Advent Road and been instructed in the school of faith.

Justin: Like?

School Zone: Like being baptized, going to Sunday school. Remember getting your Bible? Where is it, by the way?

Justin: Well, I think it's on the shelf under a pile of stuff ... awww, I realize I've sorta neglected reading it all these years.

School Zone: Yes, and there was confirmation. You made that milestone, right?

Justin: Yep, had a great day. Cake, cards, money. But listen, I go to church pretty often. Even pray once in a while.

No Passing: *(Enters)* But that's where you need me to remind you that faith doesn't get passed down. You are accountable. Everyone has to come to faith by their own confession. Not by your mom or dad or grandparent or friends or pastor. You have to answer God's call and say, "Yes," like Mary did. Advent is a great time to give God permission to move in your life once more and even more powerfully than before. For now you know. You've seen the signs. Tonight God's asking you to let Jesus come into your heart. Let's pile in. *(Enters car with School Zone)*

Kayla: *(Stands and turns to the whole group in the car)* We welcome all you signs as from God. We're almost at our destination! In fact, look! There's the new church parking lot. It's all paved and smooth. They've even got a light shining for us. *(Sits down)*

Reserved Parking Sign: *(Enters)* And here's your last sign. This spot's been reserved for you. Jesus welcomes you into the kingdom because you've prepared yourself for your faith journey. You let him cross your path and light up your life. Your thirst for more of God will now be quenched as you stop and look at your life. The rough roads have been made smooth. Yielding to God has made a difference. Now you can play and remember all you've learned. Faith isn't passed down. It grows as you daily journey with God. *(Sits down)*

Justin: *(Stands and addresses congregation)* Well, I think our journey through this night has been profitable. At least for me. I'm ready to become radical for Jesus this Advent season. How about all of you?

John: *(Comes out and talks to group and congregation)* Welcome, dear souls. It's time to receive Jesus once more. He's always there, waiting for each one of us to turn to him and receive God's love. Remember the Advent call: There's still time! Repent, turn from your sin and believe in the one who came to save you, Jesus Christ! The highway to God has been prepared. Jesus has done it all. He was born, lived, died, and rose again. And he promised to come again.

Kayla: And all God's people who have prepared for Christ's return say,

All Characters: *(Stand and speak in unison)* Amen. Come, Lord Jesus. Go in peace this Advent and love your Lord. Believe in Jesus and be born again. Amen.

Song: (Tune: We Wish You a Merry Christmas)
     Jesus, come to us this Advent.
     Jesus, come to us this Advent.
     Jesus, come to us this Advent,
     And throughout the New Year.

     Good tidings we bring to all the earth;
     God's love came at Christmas,
     And with the joy of Christ's birth.

     Jesus, come to us this Advent.
     Jesus, come to us this Advent.
     Jesus, come to us this Advent,
     And throughout the New Year.

Leader's Helps

Worship Participants: five persons
 Worship Leader
 Reader 1 — First Reading (Isaiah 40:3-5)
 Reader 2 — Second Reading (Colossians 1:15-20)
 Gospel Reader — Luke 1:5-17
 Prayer of the Day

Others:
 Prayers of the Church (Use Prayer of the Day person and three readers)
 Special music
 Pianist
 Ushers

Helps For Advent Worship Prayers Of The Church

Suggestion: Have your youth write the worship prayers to personalize them for your congregation. Sample prayers written here are by Sarah Edbauer. They may be used with her permission.

Youth #1: Now let's offer our prayers to God the Father.

(Brief silence)

God, tonight we want to pray for all of the people who are volunteering this holiday season. Keep them safe and in your light. Lord, in your mercy,
Congregation: Hear our prayer.

Youth #2: For those who are lonely. Help them to find you and your everlasting love and friendship. Lord, in your mercy,
Congregation: Hear our prayer.

Youth #3: For those who are homebound or sick during this wonderful time of year. We pray especially for those on our prayer

28

concern list *(Optional: read people on list)*, and those we name aloud or in our hearts. *(Brief silence)* Lord, in your mercy,
Congregation: Hear our prayer.

Youth #4: For our friends and family members. We're thankful for them and ask you to help them and keep them safe. Lord, in your mercy,
Congregation: Hear our prayer.

Youth #1: Hear our prayers, O Lord, and help us to remember you and your Son, Jesus Christ, this week. Help us to keep you in our every action. Amen.

Music Helps

For special music, "Come, Thou Long-Expected Jesus" (Text: Charles Wesley), use tune to "Alleluia! Sing To Jesus" (Tune: HYFRYDOL)

Opening Hymn, "Rejoice, Rejoice, Believers" (Tune: Swedish folk tune, HAF TRONES LAMPA FARDIG, 7676 D).

The Christmas Travelers

Foreword

This resource updates the journey of Mary and Joseph to Bethlehem. Join the couple as they prepare to travel from Nazareth to Bethlehem on *Salvation Airlines* Flight #123. Overhear airline clerks ask the routine questions of our travelers and be in tune with their answers. Listen as the pilots have discussion concerning preparations for the flight as well as the condition of their own lives.

Youth and teachers can make this a program to remember as they put their energy into declaring the message of Christ's birth through narration, readings, and song. This year your congregation will enjoy a Sunday school Christmas program with a unique twist. Resource comes complete with bulletin, complete script, readings, songs, and leader's helps.

The Christmas Travelers

Prelude   Youth Musicians

Welcome   Sunday School Coordinator

Opening Hymn: "Rejoice, Rejoice, Believers"
    Rejoice, rejoice, believers,
    And let your lights appear;
    The evening is advancing,
    And darker night is near.
    The bridegroom is arising
    And soon is drawing nigh.
    Up, pray and watch and wrestle;
    At midnight comes the cry.

    Our hope and expectation,
    O Jesus, now appear;
    Arise, O Sun so longed for,
    O'er this benighted sphere.
    With hearts and hands uplifted,
    We plead, O Lord, to see
    The day of earth's redemption
    That sets your people free!

Act 1: Scene 1

Time: Christmas Present
Place: Our Church
Actors: Stage Hand, Fifth Graders, and Teachers

Song: "O Christmas Tree"
Song: "Fly Away" by Lenny Kravitz
Song: "Leaving On A Jet Plane"

Act 2: Scene 1

Time: The First Christmas Eve
Place: Nazareth Airport
Actors: Joseph, Mary, Clerks
Extras: Readers, Fourth Graders

Song: "O Little Town of Bethlehem"
Song: "Oh, Come, Oh, Come, Emmanuel"

Congregational Hymn: "Oh, Come, Oh, Come, Emmanuel"
Oh, come strong Branch of Jesse, free
Your own from Satan's tyranny;
From depths of hell your people save
And give them victory o'er the grave.
Refrain: Rejoice! Rejoice! Emmanuel
Shall come to you, O Israel.

Oh, come, O Key of David, come,
And open wide our heavn'ly home;
Make safe the way that leads on high,
And close the path to misery.
Refrain

Act 2: Scene 2

Time: Pre-Boarding
Place: Interior of Flight #123
Actors: Angels, Shepherds, Pilot, Co-pilot, Stewardess
Extras: Third Graders, Reader

Song: "It Came Upon The Midnight Clear"
Song: "Hark! The Herald Angels Sing"

Congregation Hymn: "Hark! The Herald Angels Sing"
Christ, by highest heav'n adored,
Christ, the everlasting Lord,
Late in time behold him come,
Offspring of a virgin's womb.

Veiled in flesh the Godhead see!
Hail, incarnate deity!
Pleased as man with us to dwell,
Jesus, our Emmanuel!
Refrain: Hark! The herald angels sing,
"Glory to the newborn king!"

Hail the heav'n born Prince of Peace!
Hail the sun of righteousness!
Light and life to all he brings,
Ris'n with healing in his wings.
Mild he lays his glory by,
Born that we no more may die,
Born to raise each child of earth,
Born to give us second birth.
Refrain

Congregational Hymn: "Prepare The Royal Highway"
Prepare the royal highway; The King of kings is near!
Let ev'ry hill and valley A level road appear!
Then greet the King of glory, Foretold in sacred story:
Refrain: Hosanna to the Lord,
For he fulfills God's Word!

His is no earthly kingdom; It comes from heav'n above.
His rule is peace and freedom And justice, truth, and love.
So let your praise be sounding For kindness so abounding:
Refrain

Act 2: Scene 3

Time: Boarding
Place: Flight #123
Actors: Pilot, Co-pilot, Stewardess, Mary, and Joseph
Extras: First and Second Graders, Pre-K and Kindergartners

Song: "Oh, Come, All Ye Faithful"
Song: "The First Noel"

34

Congregational Hymn: "The First Noel"
    And by the light of that same star
    Three Wise Men came from country far;
    To seek for a king was their intent,
    And to follow the star wherever it went.
    Refrain: Noel, Noel, Noel, Noel!
    Born is the King of Israel.

    This star drew near to the northwest,
    O'er Bethlehem it took its rest;
    And there it did both stop and stay
    Right over the place where Jesus lay.
    Refrain

Congregational Hymn: "Oh, Come, Little Children"
    Oh, come, little children, oh, come, one and all,
    To Bethlehem haste to the manger so small.
    God's Son for a gift has been sent you this night
    To be your Redeemer, your Joy and Delight.

    He's born in a stable for you and for me;
    Draw near by the bright, gleaming starlight to see,
    In swaddling clothes lying, so meek and so mild,
    And purer than angels — the heavenly Child.

    See Mary and Joseph, with love-beaming eyes,
    Are gazing upon the rude bed where He lies,
    The shepherds are kneeling, with hearts full of love,
    While angels sing loud alleluias above.

Song: "Joy To The World"
Song: "We've Got The Joy Of Jesus Down In Our Hearts"

Act 3: Scene 1

Time: None Too Soon!
Place: Bethlehem Airport
Actors: All Participants
Extras: All Groups

Song: "Away In A Manger"

Congregational Hymn: "Joy To The World"
Joy to the world, the Lord is come!
Let earth receive its King;
Let ev'ry heart prepare him room
And heav'n and nature sing
And heav'n and nature sing,
And heav'n, and heav'n and nature sing.

Joy to the earth, the Savior reigns!
Let all their songs employ,
While fields and floods, rocks, hills, and plains
Repeat the sounding joy,
Repeat the sounding joy,
Repeat, repeat the sounding joy.

No more let sin and sorrow grow
Nor thorns infest the ground;
He comes to make his blessings flow
Far as the curse is found,
Far as the curse is found,
Far as, far as the curse is found.

He rules the world with truth and grace
And makes the nations prove
The glories of his righteousness
And wonders of his love,
And wonders of his love,
And wonders, wonders of his love.

All Groups and Participants: "Silent Night, Holy Night"
Youth
Silent night, holy night! All is calm, all is bright
Round yon virgin mother and child.
Holy Infant, so tender and mild,
Sleep in heavenly peace, Sleep in heavenly peace.

36

Youth and Congregation: "Silent Night, Holy Night"
Silent night, holy night! Shepherds quake at the sight;
Glories stream from heaven afar,
Heav'nly hosts ... sing, Alleluia!
Christ, the Savior, is born! Christ, the Savior, is born!

Silent night, holy night! Son of God, love's pure light
Radiant beams from your holy face
With the dawn of redeeming grace,
Jesus, Lord, at your birth,
Jesus, Lord, at your birth.

Youth and Congregation: "We Wish You A Merry Christmas"
We wish you a merry Christmas;
We wish you a merry Christmas;
We wish you a merry Christmas
and a happy New Year.

Good tidings to you
wherever you are;
Good tidings for Christmas
and a happy New Year!

We wish you a merry Christmas;
We wish you a merry Christmas;
We wish you a merry Christmas
and a happy New Year.

Recessional: "Go Tell It On the Mountain"
Refrain: Go tell it on the mountain,
Over the hills and ev'rywhere;
Go tell it on the mountain
That Jesus Christ is born!

While shepherds kept their watching
O'er silent flocks by night,
Behold, throughout the heavens
There shone a holy light.
Refrain

The shepherds feared and trembled
When, lo, above the earth
Rang out the angel chorus
That hailed our Savior's birth.
Refrain

Down in a lonely manger
The humble Christ was born;
And God sent us salvation
That blessed Christmas morn.
Refrain

Complete Resource

The Christmas Travelers

Prelude   Youth Musicians

Welcome   Sunday School Coordinator

Opening Hymn: "Rejoice, Rejoice, Believers"
    Rejoice, rejoice, believers,
    And let your lights appear;
    The evening is advancing,
    And darker night is near.
    The bridegroom is arising
    And soon is drawing nigh.
    Up, pray and watch and wrestle;
    At midnight comes the cry.

    Our hope and expectation,
    O Jesus, now appear;
    Arise, O Sun so longed for,
    O'er this benighted sphere.
    With hearts and hands uplifted,
    We plead, O Lord, to see
    The day of earth's redemption
    That sets your people free!

Act 1: Scene 1
(Two stagehands from the fifth grade come out with sign. Stagehand #1 holds up sign: Act 1: Scene 1, Christmas Eve, [year])

Stagehand #2: We're free! We're free! As believers in Christ we rejoice that we are free! But look! Here's a group coming in from a night of Christmas Eve caroling.

(Stagehands join their class to sing. Fifth graders enter carrying Christmas trees and singing. Two teachers are with them. Costumes: hats, mittens, scarves. One youth has CD player with headphones on and is dancing to the tune he is listening to. Readers 1-5 can be selected from this class)

Group #1: "O Christmas Tree"
O Christmas tree, O Christmas tree, how lovely are your branches.
O Christmas tree, O Christmas tree, how lovely are your branches.

(All speaking boys and girls can go to the lectern to speak)

Boy #1: No, that's not right. It's "thy leaves are so unchanging." Let's try it again.

(Group stops and sings again with the wrong words)

Group #1: "O Christmas Tree"
O Christmas tree, O Christmas tree, how lovely are your branches.
O Christmas tree, O Christmas tree, how lovely are your branches.

Teacher #1: Hey, guys! Didn't you hear John? He said you're singing the wrong words.

Girl #1: But, Mrs. Wadke, *"thy"* *(Emphasizes the word* "thy"*)* is so foreign to us. Who spoke that way, anyway?

Teacher #2: Well, that's old English. Like using "thee" and "thou" and "art" and....

Boy #2: Art? How about "herald"? Isn't *Harold* one of the angels from "Hark! It's Harold and the Angel Band"?

(Group laughs. Boy with headphones keeps dancing around, oblivious to conversation)

Teacher #1: Kyle! Hey, Kyle! *(Teacher goes up to student and takes off headphones)* Kyle! Just what Christmas song are you listening to?

Kyle: Well, Mrs. Wadke, it's not exactly a Christmas song unless you were flying someplace this Christmas vacation.

Teacher #2: Well, how about all of us hearing that song? Would your mother approve of this, Kyle?

Kyle: I think so. In fact, my class knows it and can sing it for you. Hit it, group!

(Boom box and CD — Lenny Kravitz, "Fly Away." Group dances around as tune comes on. Youth may bring out an electric guitar to mimic music. Play CD while youth mimic lyrics of first two verses as they dance)

Teacher #1: Well, that was interesting. "I want to get away ... I want to fly away ..." I can relate. I wish that I were going on a trip for Christmas. But just think of all the hassle that goes on in airports during this time.

Boy #2: I wonder what kind of trip Mary and Joseph would have had if they had flown to Bethlehem.

Girl #2: Hey, let's go downstairs and talk about that. Or maybe we all can imagine right now that we're in an airport on the night Jesus came into the world.

Girl #3: Yes, and Mary and Joseph and all the rest of our actors are leaving on a jet plane!

Boy #3: Isn't there a song about that our parents used to sing?

Teacher #2: Yes, it dates me, but I know it. And maybe you do too.

Girl #4: I think we can adapt the words to fit the time we're thinking about. Hit it, group.

Group #1: (Tune: "Leaving On A Jet Plane")
We're leaving on a jet plane
Don't know when we'll be back again.

Leaving on a jet plane
Off to the plains of Bethlehem,
O Lord, we look for you.

Leaving on a jet plane
Off to the plains of Bethlehem.
Oooooo, come fly with us!

(Group #1 leaves singing "Leaving on a jet plane, leaving on a jet plane..." Readers 1-5 sit down until their reading comes up. Stagehands sit with that group also. PA/Controller person may be seated with them also. May be an older youth or youth from fifth grade)

Act 2: Scene 1
(Stagehand #2 holds up sign: Act 2: Scene 1, Nazareth Airport)

Stagehand #1: The scene is set, and you are there. Welcome to Nazareth Airport on the eve of our Lord's birth. Let your imaginations fly as we watch our story unfold.

(Stagehands sit down behind lectern)

PA Announcement: *(From the lectern)* Flight #123 from Nazareth to Bethlehem is ready for boarding. All those with ticketed boarding passes are asked to check in at gate B.C. Make sure you have checked your bags at the appropriate spot. All carry-on luggage must be tagged. Again, all passengers flying with us today on *Salvation Airlines* from Nazareth to Bethlehem are asked to present themselves for check-in.

(All readers read from lectern and then return to their seats behind until final number)

Reader #1: This is how Jesus Christ was born. A young woman named Mary was engaged to Joseph from King David's family. But before they were married, she learned that she was going to have a baby by God's Holy Spirit (Matthew 1:18 CEV).

Joseph: *(Enters dragging a suitcase and approaches check-in counter where two clerks are behind the desk)* Hurry up, Mary! They're beginning to board our flight. We need to make sure we're on board.

Mary: *(Enters behind Joseph carrying a backpack or large diaper bag with stuffed animal sticking out and a manger)* I'm coming, Joseph. It's just a struggle with this extra baggage I'm carrying. *(Pats middle)* Are you sure we're supposed to be bringing this manger to Bethlehem? It's sure a funny-looking crib.

Joseph: I know, but God knows what he's doing with the props for this drama. *(Takes manger from Mary)* Here, let me help you. We need to tag this for carry-on. *(Puts manger on the counter)*

Clerk #1: Good day! Strange item for check in, but you must know what you're doing. *(Tags item and gives it back to Joseph)* There. Now make sure this fits in the overhead or under the seat. Are you flying to Bethlehem with us tonight?

Joseph: I sure am.

Clerk #1: Business or pleasure?

Joseph: This trip is strictly business, otherwise I would have stayed home with my very pregnant wife.

Clerk #1: Oh, I can see this is a little bit of an inconvenience.

Joseph: It sure is.

Clerk #2: Is this your first baby, young lady?

Mary: Yes, this will be my first child.

Clerk #2: Do you think you'll get back in time to have it at home?

Joseph: Not according to the script. Just listen to the background information.

Reader #2: About that time Emperor Augustus gave orders for the names of all the people to be listed in record books. The first records were made when Quirinius was governor of Syria. Everyone had to go to their own hometown to be listed. So Joseph had to leave Nazareth in Galilee and go to Bethlehem in Judea. Long ago Bethlehem had been King David's hometown, and Joseph went there because he was from David's family. Mary was engaged to Joseph and traveled with him to Bethlehem. She was soon going to have a baby, and while they were there, she gave birth to her first-born son. She dressed him in baby clothes and laid him on a bed of hay, because there was no room for them in the inn (Luke 2:1-7 CEV).

Clerk #1: Well, now, that's quite a story that's been recorded, but back to you, sir. You're going to Bethlehem to be taxed and taking along your young bride? Well, just listen to our Musac System sing about your point of destination.

(Group #2 — Fourth Graders — enter from side. Pianist plays traveling music until they get assembled in front of counters. Mary and Joseph step to side. One youth carries a large sign with notes all over it and holds it up: Heavenly Musac)

Group #2: "O Little Town Of Bethlehem"
O little town of Bethlehem, How still we see thee lie!
Above thy deep and dreamless sleep The silent stars go by;

Yet in thy dark streets shineth The everlasting light,
The hopes and fears of all the years Are met in thee tonight.

O holy Child of Bethlehem, Descend to us, we pray;
Cast out our sin, and enter in, Be born in us today.
We hear the Christmas angels The great glad tidings tell;
Oh, come to us, abide with us, Our Lord Immanuel!

(Traveling music while group goes and sits in front pews on right)

Reader #3: Mary was engaged to Joseph and traveled with him to Bethlehem. She was soon going to have a baby (Luke 2:5 CEV).

Clerk #2: So, Joseph, this is your wife? When are you due, Honey?

Mary: Very, very soon. In fact, can I sit down while you check Joseph in? *(Goes and sits down on a chair at the side while clerks and Joseph have dialogue)*

Clerk #1: Sure, this won't take long. I just need to ask you a few questions, Joseph. Did you pack your own bags?

Joseph: You might say that I did. God gave me an assignment, and I responded, "Yes," to his call to take Mary as my wife. So here we are, "some not-so-willing travelers" off on a real life journey with all the stuff we've packed and a little extra that's been given to us along the way.

Clerk #1: *(Looks at him and hesitantly responds)* Yes, sure, well ... Have your bags been in your possession since you packed them?

Joseph: You might say that. You see, I'm still trying to sort it all out. May I get a little personal here?

Clerk #1: It hasn't been busy, so we have time.

Clerk #2: We'd love to hear your side of this story.

(Both clerks lean forward)

Joseph: Well, this is a little out of the ordinary. You see, since Mary and I have been engaged, we were never allowed to be with each other alone. Someone was always with us. Then it gets real confusing.

Clerk #2: *(Pokes clerk #1 in the rib)* This is getting interesting. What's the confusing part for you?

Joseph: I found out she was pregnant.

Clerk #1: Oh, my!

Clerk #2: You mean she was going to have a baby, and it wasn't yours?

Joseph: Yes, so since she is a good woman, and I didn't want to embarrass her, I decided to quietly call off the wedding.

Clerk #2: But here you are, and you are husband and wife.

Joseph: That's right, and we're committed to God's course of action. You see, while I was thinking about all of this, an angel from the Lord appeared to me in a dream.

Clerk #1: You mean you were approached by a stranger and asked to carry an additional bag on your journey?

Joseph: You might say that. The angel told me not to be afraid to take Mary as my wife.

Clerk #2: And the child? Did the angel tell you whose child she was carrying?

Joseph: Yes, the child was from the Holy Spirit.

Clerk #1 and #2: *(Both look at each other and say in unison)* Oh, yeah! We've heard that one before.

Joseph: Well, look at her. How could you think she'd lie to me? She's so young and innocent. She always did what was right in the sight of God, so I trusted what the angel said was true.

Clerk #2: Did the angel tell you anything else?

Joseph: You might say that. He told me that I was to name the child "Jesus" for he was to save us from our sins.

Clerk #1: Well, if this girl was going to be my wife I'd like proof this child was of the Spirit!

Clerk #2: I remember a prophecy from the book of Isaiah about a virgin giving birth and the name that was to be given to him. Now where was that?

Reader #4: But the Lord will still give you proof. A virgin is pregnant; she will have a son and will name him Immanuel (Isaiah 7:14 CEV).

Clerk #1: What a promise! What a feat! But calling a child "Immanuel." Just what does that name mean?

Clerk #2: Hannah, don't you know your Hebrew? "Immanuel" means "Jesus" which means "the Lord saves." Hey, this child Mary's going to have might be the expected one, the one we have longed for. Look at her. She might be the mother of Messiah.

Group #2: *(Group stands and faces congregation to sing)*
   "Oh, Come, Oh, Come, Emmanuel"
   Oh, come, oh, come, Emmanuel,
   And ransom captive Israel,
   That mourns in lonely exile here
   Until the Son of God appear.

Refrain: Rejoice! Rejoice! Emmanuel
Shall come to you, O Israel.

Clerk #1: Let's have the congregation continue the singing of verses 3 and 5 of this song.

(Youth can sit down while congregation sings)

Congregation: "Oh, Come, Oh, Come, Emmanuel"
Oh, come, strong Branch of Jesse, free
Your own from Satan's tyranny;
From depths of hell your people save
And give them victory o'er the grave.
Refrain: Rejoice! Rejoice! Emmanuel
Shall come to you, O Israel.

Oh, come, O Key of David, come,
And open wide our heavn'ly home;
Make safe the way that leads on high,
And close the path to misery.
Refrain

Clerk #1: Hey, did you hear that? Someone better get a technician in here to check on our Musac system. *Salvation Airlines* does have the key — Emmanuel? The Key of David? Hmmm ... but back to our questions. Joseph, have you been approached by anyone unknown to you and asked to carry anything on board with you?

Joseph: You might say that. I'd never encountered an angel before, but that encounter sure changed my thought process. Once the angel said I was to marry Mary, I did, and here we are — on our way with *Salvation* to Bethlehem.

Mary: *(Begins to fidget and move back and forth on her chair)*
Joseph, are you done yet? I'm really getting uncomfortable.

Clerk #2: We just need to see a picture ID. *(Joseph pulls out wallet)* Hmmm ... Joseph the carpenter from Nazareth ... from the House of David. Okay. Here's your boarding pass. *(Gives him a boarding pass)* Seat 7A. It's a window seat. Will give you a great view on this starry night. And we've checked your bag all the way to Bethlehem. *(Tags bag and puts behind counter)*

Clerk #1: Next? Mary. Just step up here, my girl.

Mary: *(Moves to clerk with backpack/diaper bag. Joseph can go to the chair vacated by Mary and sit)* Thank you for listening to my husband. I know this is hard to believe, but everything he said is true.

Clerk #1: So, how about your bag? Did you pack it yourself? *(Takes bag and puts tag on it)*

Mary: You might say that. I was all set for my wedding. I had high favor in my community. Joseph had a good reputation, was considered a fine craftsman. I was looking forward to our life together. Life was set on a certain course, but then ...

Clerk #1: Yes, there are always interruptions, but not life-changing, I hope.

Mary: That's to be seen in Act 3. This is just Act 2.

Clerk #2: Well, I haven't read the end of this story, so I'll take your word for it. Okay, now, has anyone unknown to you approached you and asked you to carry on anything?

Mary: You might say that. My bridal wardrobe has been altered since Joseph and I began this journey. When the angel of the Lord came to me and asked me to become the mother of the Savior of the world, I said, "Yes." This wasn't something I had anticipated in packing in my bag for life, but since God asked, I think I can trust him to outfit me for the journey.

PA Announcement: *(Reads from the lectern)* Flight #123 from Nazareth to Bethlehem is now boarding. All those with ticketed boarding passes on *Salvation Airlines* Flight #123 are asked to check in at Gate B.C. Don't leave any of your items unattended. Check all bags at our counter. You don't want to feel overloaded in boarding our aircraft. Again ... *(Pauses)*, all passengers flying with us today from Nazareth to Bethlehem are asked to present themselves at the gate for boarding. It's almost midnight and time to get into the friendly skies.

(Pianist plays music for group to enter. Group #3 — Third Graders — enter from side where they have been sitting. Pilot and co-pilot [may be teachers of that class] enter and sit in chairs and begin fussing with an instrument panel. Microphones between them. Clerks, Mary, and Joseph go off stage. If needed airline counters and other props can be removed at this time to make room for other singing groups)

Act 2: Scene 2
(Stagehand #1 holds up sign: Act 2: Scene 2, Flight #123)

Stagehand #2: It's approaching midnight for our Christmas travelers. Their flight should be on time for it looks pretty clear out there. In fact, I see a group that will give us a pretty good report on this night. *(Both sit down as children sing)*

Group #3: "It Came Upon The Midnight Clear"
It came upon the midnight clear, That glorious song of old,
From angels bending near the earth To touch their harps of gold:
"Peace on the earth, good will to all,
From heav'n's all gracious king."
The world in solemn stillness lay To hear the angels sing.

Still through the cloven skies they come
With peaceful wings unfurled,
And still their heav'nly music floats O'er all the weary world.

50

Above its sad and lowly plains They bend on hov'ring wing.
And ever o'er its babel sounds The blessed angels sing.

Pilot: Hey, Zechariah. Did you hear that? I was just doing my radio check, and I heard a lot of singing. Listen! There it is again. *(Fusses with radio receiver)*

Group #3: "Hark! The Herald Angels Sing"
Hark! The herald angels sing,
"Glory to the newborn king;
Peace on earth, and mercy mild,
God and sinners reconciled."
Joyful, all you nations, rise;
Join the triumph of the skies;
With angelic hosts proclaim,
"Christ is born in Bethlehem!"
Refrain: Hark! The herald angels sing,
"Glory to the newborn king!"

Co-pilot: Hey, I like that music. Let's ask the congregation to join us in singing the other two verses with the children.

Congregation: "Hark! The Herald Angels Sing"
Christ, by highest heav'n adored,
Christ, the everlasting Lord,
Late in time behold him come,
Offspring of a virgin's womb.
Veiled in flesh the Godhead see!
Hail, incarnate deity!
Pleased as man with us to dwell,
Jesus, our Emmanuel!
Refrain: Hark! The herald angels sing,
"Glory to the newborn king!"

Hail the heav'n born Prince of Peace!
Hail the sun of righteousness!

Light and life to all he brings,
Ris'n with healing in his wings.
Mild he lays his glory by,
Born that we no more may die,
Born to raise each child of earth,
Born to give us second birth.
Refrain

Reader #5: That night in the fields near Bethlehem some shepherds were guarding their sheep. All at once an angel came down to them from the Lord, and the brightness of the Lord's glory flashed around them. The shepherds were frightened. But the angel said, (Luke 2:8-10a CEV) ...

Angel: *(One angel steps up to lectern and speaks)* Don't be afraid! I have good news for you, which will make everyone happy. This very day in King David's hometown a Savior was born for you. He is Christ the Lord. You will know who he is, because you will find him dressed in baby clothes and lying on a bed of hay (Luke 2:10b-12 CEV).

Reader #5: Suddenly many other angels came down from heaven and joined in praising God. They said ... (Luke 2:13 CEV)

Angels: *(All children from this group or specific angels can say)* Praise God in heaven! Peace on earth to everyone who pleases God (Luke 2:14 CEV).

Reader #5: After the angels had left and gone on board the aircraft ... *(Speaking angel goes and sits in chair arranged for plane)* Excuse me, I meant after the angels had left and gone back to heaven, the shepherds said to each other (Luke 2:15a CEV) ...

Shepherds: *(Shepherds step up to lectern and recite together)* Let's go to Bethlehem and see what the Lord has told us about (Luke 2:15b CEV).

Shepherd #1: I'm game.

Shepherd #2: So am I. Look! There's an airplane about to board for Bethlehem.

Shepherd #3: Okay, let's get on board. *Salvation Airlines*, prepare yourself. Here we come! Congregation, let's hear your voices prepare our way.

(Three shepherds go and sit on chairs in back of the airplane with the angel. Rest of the group exit during congregational singing)

Congregation: "Prepare The Royal Highway"
    Prepare the royal highway; The King of kings is near!
    Let ev'ry hill and valley A level road appear!
    Then greet the King of glory, Foretold in sacred story:
    Refrain: Hosanna to the Lord,
    For he fulfills God's Word!

    His is no earthly kingdom; It comes from heav'n above.
    His rule is peace and freedom And justice, truth, and love.
    So let your praise be sounding For kindness so abounding:
    Refrain: Hosanna to the Lord,
    For he fulfills God's Word!

Act 2: Scene 3
(Stagehand #2 stands up with sign: Act 2: Scene 3, Boarding)

Pilot: I guess they've started boarding already, Zechariah. So let's get everything set for take off. Have you made an eye check of the plane?

Co-pilot: *(Pulls out a clipboard and begins to tick off items with a pencil)* Yep, no dents. Check. All the bolts are in place. Check. Wish I could say that about my own life.

Pilot: What do you mean?

Co-pilot: Well, everything seems to be falling apart for me. I've been doing some things I shouldn't be doing, and I know God isn't pleased.

Pilot: Well, have you told God you're sorry?

Co-pilot: Not yet. *(Grabs hold of the controls)* I'm still in control of my life, but I don't think my flight plan and God's line up yet.

Control Tower: *(Reads from the lectern. Can be the PA person or another youth)* Control tower to Flight #123. Have you checked out your flight plan?

Pilot: We're discussing that right now, Control. How's the weather out there?

Control Tower: It's a clear night except for that light show we just had. Any idea what all that singing was about?

Pilot: A heavenly disturbance of some sort. Over and out. But let's get back to our checklist.

Co-pilot: *(Returns to check off list)* Right. Gas is okay. No oil problem ... except in my own life. I need some fuel for my journey. Maybe a Holy Spirit infusion and anointing.

Pilot: Well, dear friend, I know that since I let God take control of my life, things have run a lot smoother. Let's finish our pre-flight inventory. Have you checked the weather out there? We need to be faithful to our calling.

(Group #4 — First and Second Graders — enter to piano music. Star person leads. Three kings stand next to her)

Pilot: Hey, check this group out. We've got some strange passengers coming on board tonight.

Group #4: "Oh, Come, All Ye Faithful"
Oh, come, all ye faithful, Joyful and triumphant!
Oh, come ye, oh, come ye, to Bethlehem;
Come and behold him Born the king of angels:
Refrain: Oh, come, let us adore him,
Oh, come, let us adore him,
Oh, come, let us adore him, Christ the Lord!

Sing, choirs of angels, Sing in exultation,
Sing, all ye citizens of heaven above!
Glory to God In the highest:
Refrain

Pilot: Wow! Did you see those unidentified flying objects out there in the sky? There sure is a lot of strange traffic above this airport. Zechariah, what's that I see appearing in the sky over there? Is it a star? *(Star raised and lowered from group)* Now where in the world did that come from?

Group #4: "The First Noel"
The first Noel the angel did say
Was to certain poor shepherds in fields as they lay;
In fields where they lay, keeping their sheep,
On a cold winter's night that was so deep.
Refrain: Noel, Noel, Noel, Noel!
Born is the King of Israel.

They looked up and saw a star
(A star raised up higher from group)
Shining in the east beyond them far;
And to the earth it gave great light,
And so it continued both day and night.
Refrain

Pilot: Well, I don't know about that star, but let's keep this group boarding so we can make Bethlehem on time.

Co-pilot: *(Refers to clipboard)* According to the manifest we only have a few more passengers left. Let's check it out with our stewardess. Hey, Elizabeth, come here a minute, would you?

Elizabeth: *(Enters and picks up one of the mikes)* Yes, sirs, what can I do for you?

Pilot: Good evening, Elizabeth. We were just discussing the variety of passengers on this flight. Have you noticed anything strange?

Elizabeth: You might say that. First there was that heavenly being that boarded. A big guy with flowing robe, harp, and illuminating personality. Then came those shepherds. Don't worry. We asked them to cage their sheep and goats.

Co-pilot: So, that's what that racket is about. All that baahing ... I thought it was static. The air tonight seems to be filled with a lot of electricity, as if the whole world was waiting in anticipation of some grand event.

Elizabeth: You feel it too? Hey! *(Notices the star)* Is that a star I see? Those passengers from the East that were in the gate area were talking about a star they were following.

Pilot: What did they look like?

Elizabeth: These guys are flying first class! They're royalty, three kings, I think. When I saw them they had some costly gifts they were bringing to another king. Do you think that could be the star they're following? *(Points at the star. Star person holds star higher)*

Pilot: Well, let's ask the congregation to fill in that information with those stanzas from our next song.

(Group #4 departs led by star person. Leaves three kings who carry gifts and take their seats in front of angel and shepherds. Star person leads group back to seats on the side)

Congregation: "The First Noel"
> And by the light of that same star
> Three Wise Men came from country far;
> To seek for a king was their intent,
> And to follow the star wherever it went.
> *Refrain:* Noel, Noel, Noel, Noel!
> Born is the King of Israel.

> This star drew near to the northwest,
> O'er Bethlehem it took its rest;
> And there it did both stop and stay
> Right over the place where Jesus lay.
> *Refrain*

PA Announcement: *(Reads from lectern)* Last call for Flight #123 from Nazareth to Bethlehem. All passengers with confirmed tickets on *Salvation Airlines* are now asked to be on board.

Pilot: You'd better go out there and check your cabin, Elizabeth. Let's fire up those engines, Zechariah.

Elizabeth: Okay, but I just saw a donkey, some cattle, and doves being loaded. Do you think Hollywood's filming a special event in Bethlehem this week?

Pilot: Well, the night is now silent from what I've observed, but you never know what's going to happen on this flight plan when God is directing the action.

Co-pilot: I'm beginning to see that. Go out and give your safety talk, Elizabeth. I see your last two passengers walking our way: a man with a very pregnant wife beside him. He's certainly going to have his hands full. I hope there's a doctor on board, just in case.

(Elizabeth moves to welcome Mary and Joseph who come on board with their manger. Stay standing)

Elizabeth: Good evening. Just be seated wherever you like. We don't have a full manifest tonight.

Joseph: And where do you want me to put this crib?

Elizabeth: Crib? All I see is a wooden manger. That feeding trough for animals couldn't possible be your crib, could it?

Mary: Hmmm ... I'm sure God knows what he's doing. *(Grabs her middle)* Ooh, I think we'd better hurry, Joseph. It's nearing the time for this little one to enter the world. Maybe the congregation can help bring some of their little ones on so we can speed up the action or we might have to do some flashbacks after the fact!

Elizabeth: I agree. We'd all better sit down now so we can take off. Make sure you're all buckled up. Listen, I hear singing. It sounds beautiful.

(Mary and Joseph sit down. Joseph puts manger under chair. All pretend to buckle up. Group #5 — Pre-K and Kindergartners — enter as congregation sings. Elizabeth stays standing as she prepares to greet this group)

Congregation: "Oh, Come, Little Children"
Oh, come, little children, oh, come, one and all,
To Bethlehem haste to the manger so small.
God's Son for a gift has been sent you this night
To be your Redeemer, your Joy and Delight.

He's born in a stable for you and for me;
Draw near by the bright, gleaming starlight to see,
In swaddling clothes lying, so meek and so mild,
And purer than angels — the heavenly Child.

See Mary and Joseph, with love-beaming eyes,
Are gazing upon the rude bed where He lies,
The shepherds are kneeling, with hearts full of love,
While angels sing loud alleluias above.

Elizabeth: Well, these final passengers look like a joyful bunch. Children, what do you have to add to our message tonight as we make our way from Nazareth to Bethlehem? *(Sits down in chair on the side)*

Group #5: "Joy To The World"
Joy to the world, the Lord is come!
Let earth receive its King;
Let ev'ry heart prepare him room
And heav'n and nature sing
And heav'n and nature sing,
And heav'n, and heav'n and nature sing.

Elizabeth: *(Stands)* Thank you, young people, for making our flight from Nazareth to Bethlehem go by so fast. *(Looks at watch)* My word, we're ready to put down. Fasten your seat belts. *(Elizabeth sits down. All pretend to buckle up. Move in jerking motion)*

Group #5: (Tune: "I've Got The Joy, Joy, Joy Down In My Heart")
We've got the joy of Jesus down in our hearts,
Down in our hearts, down in our hearts.
We've got the joy of Jesus down in our hearts,
Down in our hearts, this Christmas Day.

And we're so happy, so very happy;
We've got the love of Christmas in our hearts.
And we're so happy, so very happy;
We've got the love of Christmas in our hearts.

Act 3: Scene 1

(Stagehand #1 holds up sign: Act 3: Scene 1, Bethlehem Airport. Stagehand #2 reads from lectern)

Stagehand #2: Welcome to Bethlehem, Christmas travelers. Our play is about over, but I think you all know the ending. If you don't, I'm sure you'll soon discover it.

Mary: *(Grabs middle and moans)* Oooooh, and it can't be too soon. Joseph, quickly, grab the manger and let's find that inn. I hope you made advance registrations.

Joseph: Don't worry, Mary. Everything is ready for God's Son to be born. Children, how about rehearsing a little lullaby and joining us down at the baggage claim area? Quickly, Mary! Let's go.

(Mary hops up from chair. Joseph gathers up manger. Couple disappears while youth sing)

Group #5: "Away In A Manger"
    Away in a manger, no crib for his bed,
    The little Lord Jesus laid down his sweet head;
    The stars in the sky looked down where he lay,
    The little Lord Jesus asleep on the hay.

    The cattle are lowing; the poor baby wakes,
    But little Lord Jesus no crying he makes.
    I love you, Lord Jesus; look down from the sky
    And stay by my cradle till morning is nigh.

Sunday School Superintendent: *(Enters from side)* Thank you, children, and now I ask all the youth to return so that we can sing "Silent Night." Congregation, join us in singing the rest of the verses to "Joy To The World" as our youth reassemble for their final song.

Congregation: "Joy To The World"
Joy to the earth, the Savior reigns!
Let all their songs employ,
While fields and floods, rocks, hills, and plains
Repeat the sounding joy,
Repeat the sounding joy,
Repeat, repeat the sounding joy.

No more let sin and sorrow grow
Nor thorns infest the ground;
He comes to make his blessings flow
Far as the curse is found,
Far as the curse is found,
Far as, far as the curse is found.

He rules the world with truth and grace
And makes the nations prove
The glories of his righteousness
And wonders of his love,
And wonders of his love,
And wonders, wonders of his love.

(All youth return to the front to sing "Silent Night." Joseph and Mary return carrying a baby Jesus wrapped in blanket)

Sunday School Superintendent: And now our youth will sing the first verse of "Silent Night," and then we ask the congregation to join in the rest of the verses. And as you do, remember that first Christmas night, the night in which Jesus was born.

All Youth: "Silent Night, Holy Night"
Silent night, holy night! All is calm, all is bright
Round yon virgin mother and child.
Holy Infant, so tender and mild,
Sleep in heavenly peace, Sleep in heavenly peace.

Youth and Congregation: "Silent Night, Holy Night"
Silent night, holy night! Shepherds quake at the sight;
Glories stream from heaven afar,
Heav'nly hosts sing, Alleluia!
Christ, the Savior, is born! Christ, the Savior, is born!

Silent night, holy night! Son of God, love's pure light
Radiant beams from your holy face
With the dawn of redeeming grace,
Jesus, Lord, at your birth; Jesus, Lord, at your birth.

Pilot: Well, this certainly has been an interesting night for our travelers.

Co-pilot: And what about us? After tonight, I'm ready for God to be in control. And look what time it is. The present: Christmas Eve! Are you ready for it, Elizabeth?

Elizabeth: I sure am, thanks to all the Christmas travelers I've met tonight.

Sunday School Superintendent: And are you ready, congregation? Go into this night with the message of God's love coming to you in the birth of Jesus Christ. Then go from here and tell others of that good news. Let your voices ring out that salvation has been born. Our youth would like to close by singing you a song from their heart. *(Lead them in "We Wish You a Merry Christmas!")*

All Youth: "We Wish You A Merry Christmas"
We wish you a merry Christmas;
We wish you a merry Christmas;
We wish you a merry Christmas
and a happy New Year.

Good tidings to you,
wherever you are;
Good tidings for Christmas
And a happy New Year!

We wish you a merry Christmas;
We wish you a merry Christmas;
We wish you a merry Christmas
and a happy New Year.

(Stagehand #1 holds up sign: The End!)

Stagehand #2: And all of the Sunday school youth and teachers celebrate the end of this year and do wish you a Merry Christmas and a happy New Year! Join us in the lounge after our final carol for a special fellowship hour. Let's sing our youth out with "Go Tell It On The Mountain."

(Youth leave as congregation sings)

Closing Carol: "Go Tell It On The Mountain"
> *Refrain:* Go tell it on the mountain,
> Over the hills and ev'rywhere;
> Go tell it on the mountain
> That Jesus Christ is born!

> While shepherds kept their watching
> O'er silent flocks by night,
> Behold, throughout the heavens
> There shone a holy light.
> *Refrain*

> The shepherds feared and trembled
> When, lo, above the earth
> Rang out the angel chorus
> That hailed our Savior's birth.
> *Refrain*

> Down in a lonely manger
> The humble Christ was born;
> And God sent us salvation
> That blessed Christmas morn.
> *Refrain*

Leader's Helps

Stagehands: May be dressed in Christmas best. Have signs by their seats to hold up.

Signs:
> Act 1: Scene 1, Christmas Eve (year)
> Act 2: Scene 1, Nazareth Airport
> Act 2: Scene 2, Flight #123
> Act 2: Scene 3, Boarding
> Act 3: Scene 1, Bethlehem Airport
> The End!

Other Signs:
> Gate B.C. — *Salvation Airlines* Flight #123 Departing Midnight. Nazareth to Bethlehem. May put at the corner of the altar rail. Sandwich board set up ideal.
> Heavenly Musac: notes on sign. Carried by Fourth Grade youth.

Other Props:
> 2 big boxes with signs on front: "God's First Choice: Salvation Airlines." Use for check in. May put a third box in front of piano bench for pilots. Check with grocery store for big white Nabisco boxes with red on. Ideal!
> CD Player with headphones
> Boom box and CD *Lenny Kravitz, 5*, Virgin Records America
> Electric guitar
> 1 piece of luggage
> Baggage tags
> Backpack or diaper bag with stuffed animal
> Small manger, collapsible if possible
> Baby doll with blanket

Interior of Airplane:
> Piano bench with control panel with knobs and wheels (Fisher Price car panel)
> Hats for pilots

Twelve chairs for pilot and co-pilot, one angel, three shepherds, three kings, Mary and Joseph, Elizabeth

Costumes/Props:

Group #1: (Fifth Grade) Hats, mittens, and scarves. Fake Christmas trees.

Clerks: White shirts or blouses with red blazers. Christmas ties or accessories. Name tags on shirts. Boarding pass. Tickets for baggage. Microphones to share between them. May be older youth or teachers.

Joseph: Dressed in a flannel shirt and blue jeans. Props: portable suitcase and wallet with ID. Portable microphone if possible.

Mary: Dressed in large tunic or pregnant top with blue jeans. Put pillow under top to give appearance of being pregnant. Props: backpack or large diaper bag with stuffed animal and manger. Baby Jesus doll in blanket for later. Portable microphone if possible.

Stagehands: Have signs 1-6 by them to hold up. Speak from lectern.

Group #2: (Fourth Grade) Wear Christmas best. One youth holds up sign, Heavenly Musac. Takes sign back to seat with him.

Group #3: (Third Grade) Angels and three shepherds.

Pilot and Co-pilot: Wear white shirts with Christmas or red ties and dark pants. Props: Control panel and captain hats, wings on chest, clipboard, paper, and pencil. May have a two-microphone system between them. Put a box like counter boxes in front of them. Piano bench with control systems in back of box.

Stewardess/Elizabeth: Wears red outfit with gold wings.

Group #4: (First and Second Grade) Christmas best, three kings, one angel, *optional shepherds. Prop: Star. Star person can be dressed as angel also.

Group #5: (Pre-K and Kindergarten) Wear Christmas best.

Star Of Wonder

Foreword

What a wonderful way to involve older youth or college students in a special Christmas Eve worship service for families. *Star of Wonder* includes a complete bulletin with a Christmas Litany, prayers, readings, and Christmas carols. A skit, "God's All Stars," involves: Starlight, Starbrite; Twinkle, Twinkle, the Little Star; a Shooting Star; and the Star of Wonder. The pastor has a part in the skit and has the opportunity to reflect on the meaning of the True Light. Another great resource for your worship collection this year!

Bulletin

Star Of Wonder

Prelude

Welcome And Announcements

Call To Worship
Pastor: We come together this wondrous night, to remember our God coming in human form. As we have followed the signs of Advent, preparing our hearts to make room for our Savior, let us pause in this night to gaze upon the star planted in the sky that heralds Christ's birth. May our hearts be filled with the wonder of God's everlasting love as we worship this night.
Congregation: We come with our offering of praise this night. We come to worship the King!

Opening Hymn: "The First Noel"
    The first Noel the angel did say
    Was to certain poor shepherds in fields as they lay;
    In fields where they lay, keeping their sheep,
    On a cold winter's night that was so deep.
    Refrain: Noel, Noel, Noel, Noel!
    Born is the King of Israel.

    They looked up and saw a star
    Shining in the east beyond them far;
    And to the earth it gave great light,
    And so it continued both day and night.
    Refrain

    And by the light of that same star
    Three Wise Men came from country far;

To seek for a king was their intent,
And to follow the star wherever it went.
Refrain

This star drew near to the northwest,
O'er Bethlehem it took its rest;
And there it did both stop and stay
Right over the place where Jesus lay.
Refrain

A Christmas Litany
Leader: That starry night, shepherds looked up and were awed at the display in the heavens above them.
Congregation: All creation rejoiced at your birth, Lord Jesus.
Leader: One star, in particular, shone brighter than any other.
Congregation: We look up to the heavens and behold the hand of God as the creator of so many awesome lights.
Leader: The Light of the World came to us in the form of a little baby.
Congregation: Child of Bethlehem, let your light shine upon us this night.
Leader: Jesus, you are called the Bright and Morning Star.
Congregation: We come to your manger and kneel in adoration.
Leader: As the star drew others to Bethlehem, so let the Holy Spirit draw us ever closer to Jesus this night.
Congregation: As wise people, help us to shine with the brightness of that first night so all may know of God's love that came in flesh to live among us.

Congregational Hymn: "Oh, Come, All Ye Faithful"
Oh, come, all ye faithful, Joyful and triumphant!
Oh, come ye, oh, come ye to Bethlehem;
Come and behold him Born the king of angels:
Refrain: Oh, come, let us adore him,
Oh, come, let us adore him,
Oh, come, let us adore him, Christ the Lord!

The highest, most holy, Light of light eternal,
Born of a virgin, a mortal he comes;
Son of the Father Now in flesh appearing!
Refrain

Prayer Of The Day

Pastor: Heavenly Father, when we consider your heavens, the work of your fingers, the moon and the stars, which you have set in place, we wonder that you are mindful of us, mere humans who need the salvation you offer to the world. Thank you for sending your Son, Jesus, as our Savior. As we grasp hold of the Word of life, may your light burn brightly through us with eternal love.
Congregation: Amen.

First Lesson: Psalm 8
O Lord, our Sovereign, how majestic is your name in all the earth! You have set your glory above the heavens. Out of the mouths of babes and infants you have founded a bulwark because of your foes, to silence the enemy and the avenger. When I look at your heavens, the work of your fingers, the moon and the stars that you have established; what are human beings that you are mindful of them, mortals that you care for them? Yet you have made them a little lower than God, and crowned them with glory and honor. You have given them dominion over the works of our hands; you have put all things under their feet, all sheep and oxen, and also the beasts of the field, the birds of the air, and the fish of the seas. O Lord, our Sovereign, how majestic is your name in all the earth! (NRSV)

Second Lesson: Micah 5:2-5
Bethlehem Ephrathah, you are one of the smallest towns in the nation of Judah. But the Lord will choose one of your people to rule the nation — someone whose family goes back to ancient times. The Lord will abandon Israel only until this ruler is born, and the rest of his family returns to Israel. Like a shepherd taking care of his sheep, this ruler will lead and care for his people by the power

and glorious name of the Lord his God. His people will live securely, and the whole earth will know his true greatness, because he will bring peace. (CEV)

Congregational Hymn: "O Little Town Of Bethlehem"
O little town of Bethlehem, How still we see thee lie!
Above thy deep and dreamless sleep The silent stars go by;
Yet in thy dark streets shineth The everlasting light,
The hopes and fears of all the years Are met in thee tonight.

For Christ is born of Mary, And, gathered all above
While mortals sleep, the angels keep
Their watch of wond'ring love.
O morning stars, together Proclaim the holy birth,
And praises sing to God the king, And peace to all the earth!

The Gospel Shines Its Light Into Our Hearts
Pastor: The Holy Gospel according to Saint Luke, the second chapter.
Congregation: Glory to you, O Lord.

The Gospel of our Lord: Luke 2:1-20
About that time Emperor Augustus gave orders for the names of all the people to be listed in record books. These first records were made when Quirinius was governor of Syria. Everyone had to go to their own hometown to be listed. So Joseph had to leave Nazareth in Galilee and go to Bethlehem in Judea. Long ago Bethlehem had been King David's hometown, and Joseph went there because he was from David's family.

Mary was engaged to Joseph and traveled with him to Bethlehem. She was soon going to have a baby, and while they were there, she gave birth to her first-born son. She dressed him in baby clothes and laid him in the hay, because there was no room for them in the inn.

That night in the fields near Bethlehem some shepherds were guarding their sheep. All at once an angel came down to them from the Lord, and the brightness of the Lord's glory flashed around them. The shepherds were frightened. But the angel said, "Don't be afraid! I have good news for you, which will make everyone happy. This very day in King David's hometown a Savior was born for you. He is Christ the Lord. You will know who he is, because you will find him dressed in baby clothes and lying on a bed of hay.

Suddenly many other angels came down from heaven and joined in praising God. They said: "Praise God in heaven! Peace on earth to everyone who pleases God."

After the angels had left and gone back to heaven, the shepherds said to each other, "Let's go to Bethlehem and see what the Lord has told us about." They hurried off and found Mary and Joseph, and they saw the baby lying on a bed of hay.

When the shepherds saw Jesus, they told his parents what the angel had said about him. Everyone listened and was surprised. But Mary kept thinking about all this and wondering what it meant.

As the shepherds returned to their sheep, they were praising God and saying wonderful things about him. Everything they had seen and heard was just as the angel had said. (CEV)

Pastor: The Gospel of our Lord.
Congregation: Praise to you, O Christ.

Congregational Hymn: "Wonder Of All Wonders" (Tune: Jesus Loves The Little Children)
(Children are invited up front during the singing of the hymn)
    Born in Bethlehem was Jesus,
    Born to set God's people free;
    The Father loved the world so much
    That he sent his son to touch
    The sinful hearts of all humanity.

    Born a light unto the nations,
    Shining down through time and space.
    Shepherds, villagers and kings
    To the Lord their praises sing:
    "Glory to the Savior of the human race!"

God placed in the sky a beacon
To show the wonder of that night.
And for all eternity
The Star of Wonder do we see
Jesus, Wonder of all wonders, come to me.

Skit: God's All Stars

(Passing out of Christmas lights)

Congregational Hymn: "There's A Star In The East"
(Children return to their seats during singing)
There's a star in the East on Christmas morn,
Rise up, shepherd, and follow.
It will lead to a place where Christ was born,
Rise up, shepherd, and follow.
Refrain: Follow, follow, rise up, shepherd, and follow,
Follow the star of Bethlehem,
rise up, shepherd, and follow.

If you take good heed to the angel's words,
Rise up, shepherd, and follow.
You'll forget your flocks, you'll forget your herds,
Rise up, shepherd, and follow.
Refrain

Pastoral Reflection

Prayers Of The Church

Receiving Of The Christmas Offering

Hymns Sung During Offering
"As With Gladness Men Of Old"
As with gladness men of old did the guiding star behold;
As with joy they hailed its light, leading onward, beaming bright;
So, most gracious Lord, may we evermore be led by thee.

As with joyful steps they sped, Savior, to thy lowly bed,
There to bend the knee before thee, whom heav'n and earth adore;
So may we with willing feet ever seek thy mercy seat.

"Angels, From The Realms Of Glory"
Angels, from the realms of glory,
Wing your flight o'er all the earth;
Once you sang creation's story;
Now proclaim Messiah's birth:
Refrain: Come and worship, come and worship,
Worship Christ, the newborn king.

Shepherds in the fields abiding,
Watching o'er your flocks by night,
God with us is now residing,
Yonder shines the infant light.
Refrain

Sages, leave your contemplations,
Brighter visions beam afar;
Seek the great desire of nations,
You have seen his natal star.
Refrain

All creation, join in praising
God, the Father, Spirit, Son,
Evermore your voices raising
To the eternal Three in One.
Refrain

Presentation Of Offering And Elements

Offertory Prayer
Pastor: Merciful Father, we offer you these gifts for your use. May
we always remember the gift you gave us of the life and death of
your precious Son, Jesus. Receive the gift of our lives to be lived
in your service. We pray in Christ's name.
Congregation: Amen.

Words Of Institution

Pastor: In the night in which he was betrayed, our Lord Jesus took bread, and gave thanks; broke it, and gave it to his disciples, saying: Take and eat; this is my body, given for you. Do this for the remembrance of me. Again, after supper, he took the cup, gave thanks, and gave it for all to drink, saying: This cup is the new covenant in my blood, shed for you and for all people for the forgiveness of sin. Do this for the remembrance of me.

The Lord's Prayer *(Unison)*

Our Father, who art in heaven,
> **hallowed be thy name.**
Thy kingdom come,
> **thy will be done,**
> **on earth as it is in heaven.**
Give us this day our daily bread;
> **and forgive us our trespasses,**
> **as we forgive those who trespass against us;**
> **and lead us not into temptation,**
> **but deliver us from evil.**
For thine is the kingdom, and the power, and the
> **glory, forever and ever. Amen**

Distribution Of Communion

Communion Hymns

> "O Holy Night"
> O holy night, the stars are brightly shining;
> It is the night of the dear Savior's birth.
> Long lay the world in sin and error pining,
> Till He appeared and the soul felt its worth.
> A thrill of hope, the weary soul rejoices,
> For yonder breaks a new and glorious morn.
> Fall on your knees, oh, hear the angel voices!
> O Night divine, O night when Christ was born!
> O Night, O holy night, O night divine!

"Angels We Have Heard on High"
Angels we have heard on high,
Sweetly singing o'er the plains,
And the mountains in reply,
Echoing their joyous strains.
Refrain: Glo ... ria in excelsis Deo;
 Glo ... ria in excelsis Deo.

Shepherds, why this jubilee?
Why your joyous strains prolong?
What the gladsome tidings be
Which inspire your heav'nly song?
Refrain

Come to Bethlehem, and see
Him whose birth the angels sing:
Come adore on bended knee,
Christ the Lord, our newborn King.
Refrain

"Away In A Manger"
Away in a manger, no crib for his bed,
The little Lord Jesus laid down his sweet head;
The stars in the sky looked down where he lay,
The little Lord Jesus asleep on the hay.

The cattle are lowing; the poor baby wakes,
But little Lord Jesus no crying he makes.
I love you, Lord Jesus; look down from the sky
And stay by my cradle till morning is nigh.

Be near me, Lord Jesus; I ask you to stay
Close by me forever and love me, I pray.
Bless all the dear children in your tender care
And fit us for heaven to live with you there.

"Joy To The World"
Joy to the world, the Lord is come!
Let earth receive its King;
Let ev'ry heart prepare him room
And heav'n and nature sing
And heav'n and nature sing,
And heav'n, and heav'n and nature sing.

Joy to the earth, the Savior reigns!
Let all their songs employ,
While fields and floods, rocks, hills, and plains
Repeat the sounding joy,
Repeat the sounding joy,
Repeat, repeat the sounding joy.

No more let sin and sorrow grow
Nor thorns infest the ground;
He comes to make his blessings flow
Far as the curse is found,
Far as the curse is found,
Far as, far as the curse is found.

He rules the world with truth and grace
And makes the nations prove
The glories of his righteousness
And wonders of his love,
And wonders of his love,
And wonders, wonders of his love.

Pastor: The body and blood of our Lord Jesus Christ strengthen you and keep you in his grace.
Congregation: Amen.
Pastor: And now may the light of Christ shine in us as we remember that Holy night when our Lord was born.

Congregational Hymn: "Silent Night, Holy Night"
>   Silent night, holy night! All is calm, all is bright
>   Round yon virgin mother and child.
>   Holy Infant, so tender and mild,
>   Sleep in heavenly peace, Sleep in heavenly peace.
>
>   Silent night, holy night! Shepherds quake at the sight;
>   Glories stream from heaven afar,
>   Heav'nly hosts sing, Alleluia!
>   Christ, the Savior, is born! Christ, the Savior, is born!
>
>   Silent night, holy night! Son of God, love's pure light
>   Radiant beams from your holy face
>   With the dawn of redeeming grace,
>   Jesus, Lord, at your birth,
>   Jesus, Lord, at your birth.

Benediction And Dismissal

Pastor: As we have worshiped our King this night, let us go in the name of the Father who created light and loves us, the Son who came as God's light to save us, and the Holy Spirit who guides and directs us to the perfect light. Go, in peace to celebrate the wonder and joy of Christmas.

Congregation: We go as wise people, drawn closer to the light of God's love and reflecting that light to the world!

Closing Hymn: "Hark! The Herald Angels Sing"
>   Hark! The herald angels sing,
>   "Glory to the newborn king;
>   Peace on earth, and mercy mild,
>   God and sinners reconciled."
>   Joyful, all you nations, rise;
>   Join the triumph of the skies;
>   With angelic hosts proclaim,
>   "Christ is born in Bethlehem!"
>   *Refrain:* Hark! The herald angels sing,
>   "Glory to the newborn king!"

Christ, by highest heav'n adored,
Christ, the everlasting Lord,
Late in time behold him come,
Offspring of a virgin's womb.
Veiled in flesh the Godhead see!
Hail, incarnate deity!
Pleased as man with us to dwell,
Jesus, our Emmanuel!
Refrain

Hail the heav'n born Prince of Peace!
Hail the sun of righteousness!
Light and life to all he brings,
Ris'n with healing in his wings.
Mild he lays his glory by,
Born that we no more may die,
Born to raise each child of earth,
Born to give us second birth.
Refrain

Skit

God's All Stars

Participants:
  Starlight, Starbrite
  Twinkle, Twinkle the Little Star
  Shooting Star
  Star of Wonder
  Pastor

Costumes/Props:
  Starlight, Starbrite: wears red star garland around head and
    neck; carries a red star wand with streamers and a flash-
    light.
  Twinkle, Twinkle: wears gold garland around neck and waist
    and gold star garland on head; carries a white star wand
    with streamers.
  Shooting Star: wears jeans, vest with stars, handkerchief
    around neck, straw cowboy hat with garland around it; car-
    ries a gold star with a long, gold garland tail.
  Star of Wonder: wears white robe with silver garland around
    neck and waist, silver star garland around head; silver star
    hangs around neck; carries large silver star with silver gar-
    land outlining it and around handle.

(Youth are invited up during the singing of the song)

Pastor: Welcome, and Merry Christmas! What a beautiful night to
celebrate the birth of the Lord Jesus. It's a special time for all ages, but
especially for children. I can tell you're all excited about Christmas.
Aren't you? When you came to church tonight, did you look up at the
heavens and wish for ways to make this Christmas special for your
family, for yourself, and for others? Do you remember that little jingle

that goes, "Star light, star bright, first star I see tonight. I wish I may, I wish I might have the wish I wish tonight"?

Starlight, Starbrite: *(Enters)* Hello, everybody! Thanks, Pastor, for wishing me down from the sky!

Pastor: And who might you be?

Starlight, Starbrite: Why I'm that first star in the sky ... *Starlight, Starbrite.* And I've been wished down here to bring you a greeting from God, the Creator of the universe. I've been shining with a great light for a loooong time! In fact, it's been since the beginning of the world, when God said, "Let there be light," and he created the sun, the moon, and all of the starry hosts. My light has shone every night since creation. *(Shines bright flashlight at youth)*

Pastor: My, you are a bright star!

Starlight, Starbrite: Not just *bright* in light, but I am also *wise.* I know the Creator of the universe, and tonight is a very special night to think about God's light.

Pastor: Why is that?

Starlight, Starbrite: Because there's been a lot of talk throughout the heavens about a new star appearing with a special announcement.

Twinkle, Twinkle: *(Enters)* You've heard about it, too? I'm a'twinkle *(Does a shakedown dance)* with joy and anticipation about this new star that's soon to appear.

Pastor: And who are you?

Twinkle, Twinkle: Why, don't you recognize me, Pastor (name)? You were gazing at me just the other night when you walked home from church. I'm "Twinkle, Twinkle, the Little Star." You were just asking how I was as you looked up at all of us stars shining like diamonds in the sky.

Pastor: Yes, I remember thinking how beautiful the heavens were that night. Stars were everywhere. It was quite a sight. God sure can put on some wonderful light shows.

Shooting Star: *(Enters)* And then you saw me and my magnificent tail! Remember, I went shooting across the sky just over the steeple of the church?

Pastor: I sure do. You must be that gorgeous shooting star that caught my eye.

Shooting Star: Yep! Not a six-shooter like in Westerns. *(Twirls star like a gun)* You see, stars have so much light and power because we are filled with cosmic energy. But then there's a time to die. That's when I blaze a path across the heavens to get humans' attention. God is always trying to grab your attention, you know. He wants you to die to yourself so you can have life in him. But you people are a tough crowd.

Twinkle, Twinkle: They sure are. God creates such wonders in the night to display his greatness. Who cannot look at the heavens and not realize that there is a great Creator of the universe to whom we should give praise?

Starlight, Starbrite: And during the day, God is always arranging ways for you to encounter him also. He wants to announce to the world how much he loves it.

Shooting Star: But God knows you humans so well. He ought to: God created you with wills to follow him or turn away. His hope is that you'll respond to his love. But people just keep following their own ways — often perishing without responding to a God who wants the whole world reconciled to him. And so God took a big step in his plans to bring you the light of his love. And all heaven is a flutter with it right now.

Twinkle, Twinkle: And we are on a team: God's All Stars. Each one of us has a part to play in God's plan. I'm to go forth and shine even more brightly over the fields of Bethlehem tonight.

Starlight, Starbrite: I'll follow, for I know there will be shepherds out there, looking up. That's when they'll see me and wonder at the majesty of God. Their prayer and wish will be that the Savior of the world would come soon.

Shooting Star: And at the appointed time, I'll appear! Blazing across the heavens with a host of angels. The sky will be filled with the wonder of God and beautiful singing. Then as they have their eyes fixed toward God, suddenly ...

Star of Wonder: *(Enters)* I will appear!

Pastor: And your name?

Star of Wonder: Why, Pastor, you've been singing a lot of songs tonight about me. I'm the *Star of Wonder*. God created me with one purpose: to announce to the world that his Son is born. And so, I am joining this wonderful cast of God's All Stars to make the declaration that Salvation has been born tonight. What wonderful good news!

Pastor: "And the light will shine in the darkness, and the darkness will not overcome it" (John 1:5).

Star of Wonder: But before we go, we want your children to have a light to shine as they remember Jesus, God's perfect light who came into our world to save it. And God continues to use each one of us as God's All Stars to be lights that shine to others. Can we give out our lights to the children as our gift this night?

Pastor: Sure, but before we do, let me share some words with our children about the light of Christmas, and then we'll pray.

Leader's Helps

Pastor may give a brief reflection on the Light of the World, Jesus. Then pray with the children.

Stars can be older youth or college-age young people who are home on break. Stars give out gift lights to children (small flashlights or other lights can be purchased). Youth return to their seats. Stars sit down when done.